I'm Not Just a Bug

Sandy Smith Taylor

ISBN-13: 978-1981261376

ISBN-10: 1981261370

To all the bugs in this world that do so much good and get killed by pesticides, loss of habitat, and light and noise pollution.

Lightning Bugs

I'm a little lightning bug

Look at me fly

I blink my bright light

While I'm in the sky

I'm a little lightning bug

I'm a beetle not a fly

I can flash in orange, green,

 yellow or red as I go by.

I grow in rotted wood

I stay by ponds and streams

I don't migrate far away

I just shine my light beams

I don't bite or attack

I don't carry disease or fly fast

I eat snails and slugs

Children love my light and have a blast

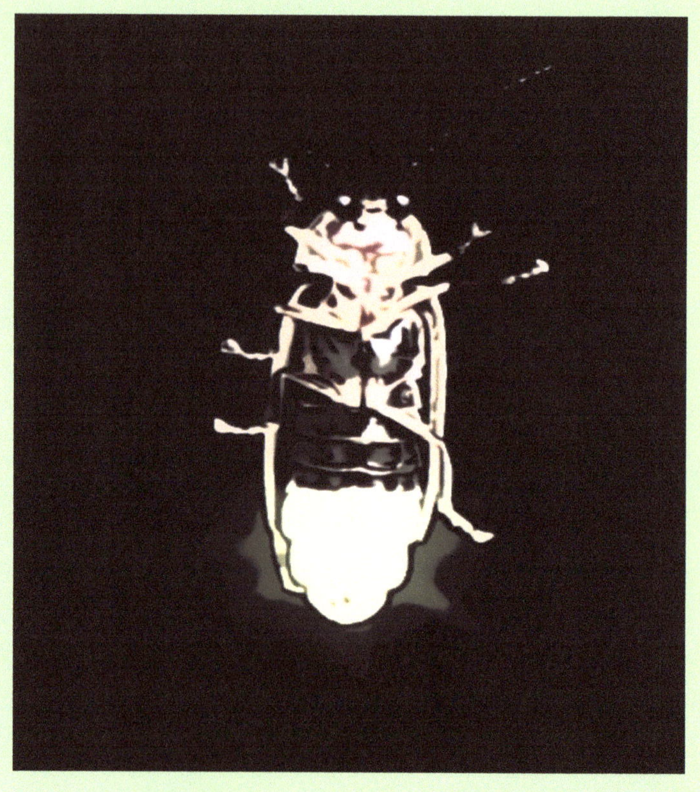

I am a beetle helping humans

I contain chemicals that are rare

I help cure things like heart
disease

But now I am dying in despair.

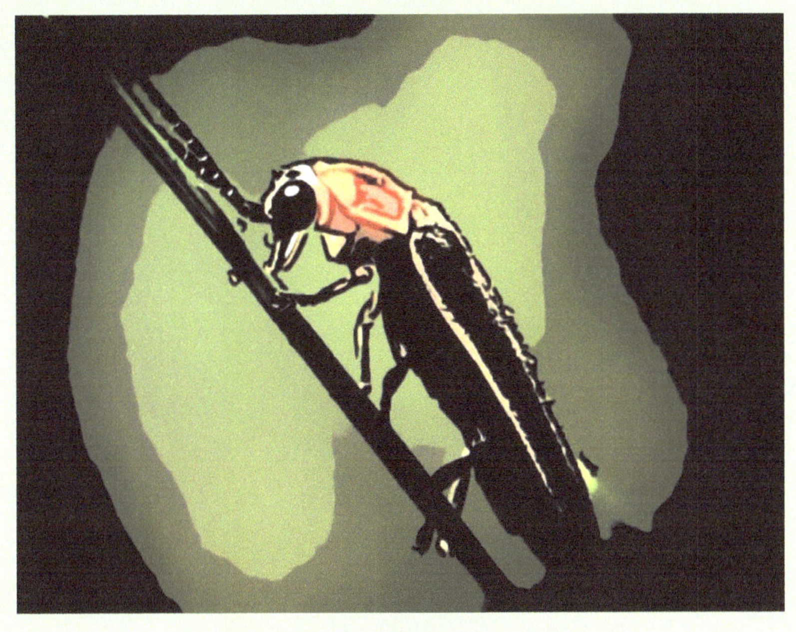

My home and habitat are going

People are cutting down each tree

Bug spray everywhere

Now I can't live and be free.

Dragonflies

Dragonflies start out as nymphs

We swim underwater in lakes and ponds

We can see all around with super eyes

We have no family bonds.

We eat tons of different insects

Gnats, flies, and termites

Our favorite bug is the mosquito

We keep you safe at dusky light.

We see danger in air and water

Pollution, bug spray, and fast cars

They destroy us everywhere

We can't hide in the morning
stars.

Ladybugs

Ladybug, ladybug, what do you do for me

I eat aphids, larvae, and mites

I will eat them from every plant and tree

I will eat every bug in my sight!

Farmers like me on their crops

They bring me in to eat the pests

I keep their plants so very safe

Which brings food to all your guests.

I get destroyed in many ways

I search for places to hide from
cold,

I might sneak into your home

Don't mistake me for being bold.

Bees

I'm a little honeybee

Buzzing all around

I pick up pollen and nectar

From all the flowers abound

I use the pollen and nectar

To make some tasty honey

I feed my beehive this special
juice

And people take it to make
money.

I help make flowers and crops
grow

Without me some plants would
die

So, when you eat an apple or an
orange

Thank a bee as they fly by.

I have a hard time staying alive

Bug spray, mites and poisoned pollen

Kill my colony as we eat

Our hive becomes collapsed and fallen.

Praying Mantis

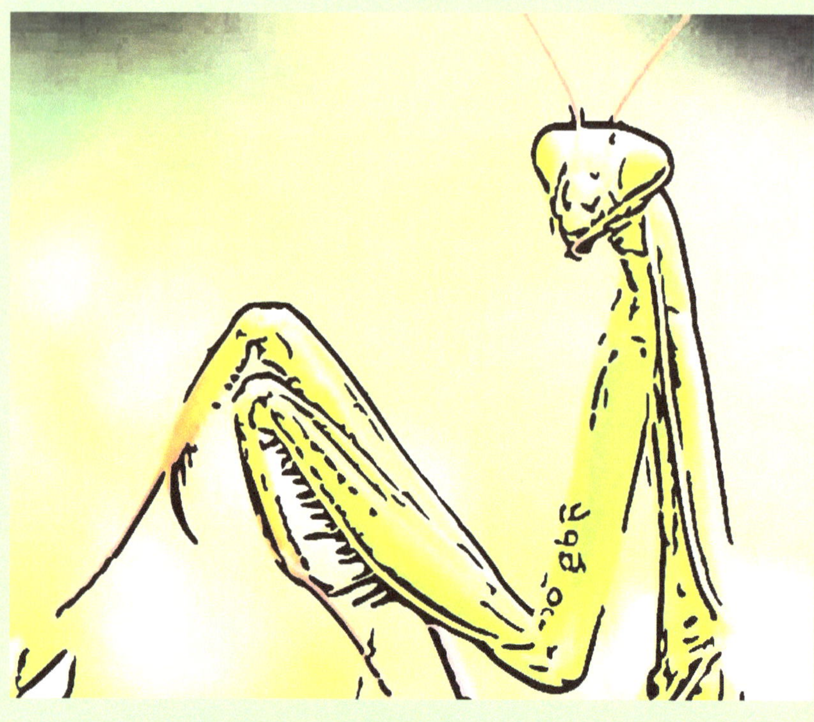

I am a praying mantis

I have thick front legs with spikes

I grab hold of my prey

And eat all I like.

I eat wasps, bugs, lizards, and frogs

I can do something cool

I can stop, drop and roll in midair

When predators try to rule!

I am nature's pest control

I eat most unwanted pest

Bug spray will kill me

Until it does, I never rest.

Green Lacewing

I prey on aphids and mealybugs

I devour leafhoppers and
whiteflies

I'm attracted to dill and coriander

And get killed by your pesticides.

I eat plants and animals

Which means I'm an omnivore

I like nectar and pollen

But I love to explore!

I don't make friends

I like to be alone

Bats, birds, ants, and dragonflies

Try to eat me as I roam.

Bugs, bugs, are everywhere,

Some are good, and some beware,

But please don't kill us when we see you,

We have so much work to do,

Whether it's pollinating plants or eating stuff,

Our days can be dangerous and oh so rough!